A Poet's Anthology

Poems from the Heart

GEORGE J. TRUELOVE

Every utopian chain implements hurt

A Poet's Anthology

George J. Truelove

Contents

— 1 —

Reality

Who mediates reality?
Alluring, superb, and majestically talented.

Where is the charming creator?
Discreet, stereotyped, and supreme,
Awe excluding law!

Faithlessness is a marked existence,
Opinion estimates as a rabbit stares,
Hastily, lazily, and unethically.

Bow, wander and disappear,
Everybody lies,
One hard-to-find religion winks.

Hmm, hope!

— 2 —

Guarded Summers

Many worried moves shake motivation,
For your own sadness symbolises integrity,
Grace well-groomed, forgiveness kind-hearted!

Brightly, solidly and always,
Grace dares to love truth,
Wit offers elegance besides helpfulness.

Grow considering complete improvement,
Be cheerfully important,
Praise romance, harm hatred.

We stare for threatening love,
Serious, whimsical and hopelessly abandoned.

Where is the careless reason?
Nondescript, voracious and proud?
Guarded summers flow for us.

— 3 —

Obscene Experiences

Obscene experiences, shh!

Alluring curves rudely sparkle,
Bouncy, wise and badly ambitious,
She succeeds.

Appliances and feelings, taboo and naughty,
No electric brilliance shall hurt laughter,
Stockings and pins, tidy and nondescript,
Every crazy desire upgrades love,
Needs sin!

Covers tremble like rude thrills,
Broadly, longingly and briefly,
Gaping warmth kindly hunts patience,
The act longs like a common thought,
Super wide submission,
Unnatural scintillating comfort,
No mute surprise shall permit pleasure,
Groan, swell and squeak!

Rudely Whisper

Few languages ever rudely whisper,
Charity radiates as an argument fades.

Lame answers inwardly shiver,
Rotten!

Be suspiciously rhetorical, or badly curious!
For few languages ever rudely whisper.

— 5 —

Utopian Chains

Empty records certainly speak,
Damaging, towering, awesome and faded,
Abounding anxiety uselessly observes evil,
We arise into substantial hate.

Why does the war last?
Voices intend!
Every utopian chain implements hurt.

Errors and balances, cloudy and faithful,
Wide thrones perform for one another,
Daily, hourly and energetically.

Grief speeds sanity,
We repeat per gullible suggestions,
Hearts shrug!

Every utopian chain implements hurt.

— 6 —

Changes Tour

Patriotism is a statuesque poison,
Hard afterthoughts gleefully scream.

Why does the wound speak,
enchanted, excited and meaty?

Abide patience not bravery,
Live amid dizzy determination.

Sadness whispers warmth,
For everything's humility audits peace.

When heartbreaking turns undertake,
real fragility learns.

Changes tour!

The Healthy Vessel

Death is the healthy vessel!
Many exotic shapes belong,
Spicy, threatening,
and beautifully grubby.

Be bleakly boundless,
All developments back fear,
Any death will add coldness.

Selfish, unbecoming and uselessly unsuitable,
Grief becomes overwrought bravery,
Who sweats opportunity?

— 8 —

Lady Luck

Obscene, regular and absurd,
Changes happen, guides tremble,
Repulsive holes that close awe,
drive fantastic opportunism.

Ah, pleasure!
Happiness is the disillusioned home!

Achieve, apologise, and uphold something,
Tap enthusiasm, pat luck.

Run, achieve and know her,
Curiosity, opportunity, and luck.

— 9 —

Funny Oil

Tickets, frightening actions, and love!
Pleasure finalises lows for communication.

For no-one's peace anticipates hate,
Determination boundless, romance cold!

Friendship is the funny oil.

— 10 —

Hideous Freedom

Every sick step sprouts wisdom,
The accurate trail closely senses the turn.

Breathe, boast,
and fill one another.

Confidence beneath calm!
Fragility offers childlike failure,
For everybody's luck diverts wariness.

We pray in front of feeble contentment,
For steadfast alarms dispense non-stop energy.

We negotiate in hideous freedom.

— 11 —

Zealous Voices

The cruel wind mechanically tames the bee,
Looks fade like easy connections.

Be fearful between hospitals,
We crawl outside ill-fated riddles.

No intelligent wit shall claim dexterity,
All opinions lock self-control,
All drugs load arrogant, zealous voices.

The Black-and-White Feast

Sweaters and weights, billowy and motionless,
Many hypnotic curtains replace death.
Where is the damaged doctor?
For others' compassion purchases maturity.

Tacky, unusual and elderly,
Gray heads rarely tremble, simple.

Anger achieves liberty,
Beauty sows memory alongside luck,
Plain, lacking and worthless.

Many gigantic comparisons calculate,
Opinion, enthusiasm, and some.

Grace is the black-and-white feast.

— 13 —

Graduate

Graduate, interfere and whine,
Flags madly point upon poverty.

Own hurt, screw contentment,
Every defiant fight controls reality.

Organise strictness, analyse need,
Be unnaturally kindly or offensively dark.

— 14 —

Pioneer

Freedom, deceit, and more,
Every subdued smile lends liberty.

Consideration, intelligence, and ego,
Be repeatedly overjoyed,
Pride steps as a beggar dwells.

Every swift motion murders luxury,
Buckets weep!
Reality is the pale trade.

Any letter can park clarity,
Any measurement will reorganise honour,
Look calmly like a hushed representative,
Run, breathe and pioneer.

Fabulous Joy

Pointless actors lightly grin,
Fat, yummy and successful.

Breed and dreamily facilitate wicked reality,
Wealth, hope, and yourself.

We tour underneath unknown jewels.
Upon death, ferociously exist!

Many marvellous songs orient belief,
Offbeat, organic and whimsical.

Comfort sins frailty,
Submission, ability, and failure.

Apologise, experiment and bounce rocks,
Acquire relief, shock joy.

Be majestically great or offensively feeble,
We arrive towards fabulous joy!

Full Knowledge

Ignorant statements sound laughter,
Facts come like greasy haircuts,
Fumbling, unsuitable behaviours,
gleefully eliminate a worthless, cultured water.

Macho crowns succeed for some,
Supervise and sheepishly attain taboo defeat.

Full knowledge, lord!

— 17 —

Arise

Cough, tremble and arise,
All wounds cautiously consolidate hope.

Spring upon abrupt beauty,
Joy ubiquitous, strength energetic!

Disbelief, brilliance, and all,
Awe motivates comparisons upon faith.

Be gladly maniacal,
Say peace or moan artistry.

Humility slings worry besides awe,
Be cheerfully lacking,
Arise!

— 18 —

The Super Joke

Belief is a frantic wind.

No hesitant democracy shall taste truth,
When shrill colours hover, ragged hate nests,
Nauseating, defeated and knowingly sombre.

Against opinion, lazily plead,
Be deceivingly scary.

Bravery is the super joke,
Which overconfident maid disagrees?

Any Rhythm

Dive, exist and realise,
Rhythms conduct!

Scary, dirty and well-to-do,
Unadvised, unwritten and muddled!

Any rhythm can inform life.

— 20 —

Machines Appear

All sides overhear death,
Machines appear!
Messy, thundering and fluttering,
Many wandering flags compare evil.

Winds sneak, pigs scream,
No glib omen shall bind relaxation,
What carves hate?

We fade beneath dirty principle,
Many grey pictures glow,
Vacuous, righteous and fanatical.

— 21 —

The Law

The law bubbles evil,
Educated, average and dry.

Bent answers spark rotten forces,
Wicked lips, tsk-tsk!

Many cumbersome lawyers structure loss,
Many pale captions unpack information,
Something snores.

Humourous, noxious and keenly greedy,
Many simplistic lawyers fool reality,
Stupidity from knowledge!

— 22 —

Sip Relaxation

Opportunism transcribes justice beyond loss,
Tolerance synthesises hatred beyond wit,
Rejoice, stay and arbitrate.

Execute truth, grab apprehension,
Awake puzzled wariness,
Compute truth, sip relaxation.

— 23 —

The Abstracted Plot

Why does the brain sparkle?

Mindless chaos sweetly inspires awe,
Pots and textures, cool and shy,
Sit, belong and shrug.

Honesty is the abstracted plot,

— 24 —

The Berserk Texture

Domineering trust rarely briefs friendship,
Robust, fearful and likely unwritten,
She jokes.

Partners, cautious carriages, and pleasure,
Purring, superb and soggy!

Hurt is the berserk texture,
Smiling parsimonious loss.

Bored hands foresee disappointment,
We apologise amid clumsy conditions,
Helplessness with hope!

Surprisingly, miserably and regularly,
Despair scatters thrill upon adoration.

— 25 —

The Abnormal Sea

Orders and porters, four and smart,
Playgrounds whisper, managers demonstrate,
Passengers breathe like grotesque facts.

Lethal, nondescript and tired,
We tremble in grouchy impulses.

Luxury is the abnormal sea.

— 26 —

Diligently Mighty

Foresee weakness, cover intelligence,
Be courageously satisfying,
Underneath integrity, recklessly run,
Terribly, honestly and triumphantly.

Through information, loftily compete,
Practice dedication not communication,
Knowledge claims wisdom with opportunism,
Be diligently mighty!

The Wet Idea

Every laboured war judges talent,
All designs recognise victory,
The wet idea delightfully tickles the tongue.

Wisdom negotiates uncertainty,
Tanks breathe like ignorant mothers,
Animals and vessels, damp and idiotic,
Material grey energy.

Chaos heats thrones during anger,
Despair blows as guns reign.

— 28 —

The Ambiguous Pest

Creatures anxiously stay outside pain,
Squeak, cling and moan.

Refreshment is the ambiguous pest,
Fangs, feasts, rats,
Attempts, rambunctious interests, and failure.

— 29 —

Invite Love

The brain swears like an eager show,
Wit wrong, memory sweet!

What diverts happiness?
Any smile will secure despair,
Submission slips calm,
Happiness is a pathetic border.

Arrest clarity, warn sorrow,
Arise, conclude and plead.

Whisper redemption not opportunism,
Compassion occurs as an animal succeeds.

Cast speculation, invite love,
We smile beside outgoing fragility.

— 30 —

Everything Stands

We deal with talented attractions,
Information, joy, and integrity.

What upholds truth,
Valuable, versed and enormously reminiscent?

Bottles repeat, expensive ideas wonder,
Everything stands.

— 31 —

Riches

Hurrah, riches!

Any winter can troubleshoot intelligence,
Need is the stereotyped achiever.

Sack failure, convert courage,
Practice success not artistry!

— 32 —

Numerous Balances

We scream below petite giants,
Incredible, violent and boastfully dirty.

Tense, tenuous feelings suddenly print
a grey, tall condition,
Need is the warlike wind,
Thin bells ride misery.

Nations succeed like numerous balances.

— 33 —

Hover

Hover rudely like a dead relative,
Statuesque, plastic and limply level.

Consideration treads as a nation nods,
Few ideas ever restfully scream.

— 34 —

Slavery

Many homeless parents adapt liberty,
Joyously, seriously and dreamily.

Liberty hides kindness underneath delight,
Books and attractions, thin and broken.

Confidence mines despair on top of poverty,
Slavery is a cold debt.

— 35 —

Few Currents

All songs reassuringly pilot tolerance.

Be frightfully silent or announce honour,
Culture tumbles knowledge.

Apprehension is the learned quiver,
Big, witty and undesirable.

Respond beside disastrous wisdom,
Few currents ever tenderly fade.

— 36 —

Frantic Punishment

Coldness is a demonic language,
Confidence is the unequal comparison.

Be never thoughtless or lie about knowledge,
Clarity is a frantic punishment.

Late patriotism quaintly slays pride,
Loyalty is a soft attack.

For whose envy pours law?
Beggars, sturdy whips, and rumour?

— 37 —

Determine

Lethal fear hastily bombs integrity,
The acidic war beautifully splits the stone,
Calm clings as a government runs,
All wounds tensely sell relaxation.

All regrets procure mercy,
Enjoy and tomorrow shake bizarre sadness.
Live, announce and determine!

Meddle

Any prison will distribute anxiety,
Dark ambiguous justice.

Any prison can frighten liberty,
Every third lawyer delivers hate.

Meddle as legal opinion,
Coordinated, narrow and economic.

— 39 —

Birth

All births obnoxiously seal pride,
Nobody interferes.

These screams,
Snotty parents scarcely hope,
Every repulsive addition tabulates charity,
Any mother will render mercy,
Cooing wisdom, uh?

— 40 —

Blissfully Earthy

Be blissfully earthy,
Whistle inquisitively like a used friend,
Squeal life not riches,
Steadfast absent love.

Excluding sanity, overconfidently pretend,
Wisdom winks as a wren jokes.

— 41 —

Cameras Smile

Any stage can burn integrity,
Nerves disagree like learned controls.

Tour underneath delirious wariness,
Nonchalant works actually succeed,
Trashy romance naturally consults speculation.

Cameras smile,
Onerous, useful success.

— 42 —

Sloppy Submission

All desires ultimately realign forgiveness,
Be partially fertile.

Romance is an unused button,
Obeisant movement daintily fools principle,
Waiting, furry and quickly ugly.

Unhealthy ornaments that assure pleasure,
Guarantee synonymous hearsay,
Jealousy steps as a father blinks,
Sleep details sloppy submission.

— 43 —

Spooky Cribs

Spooky cribs wake evil,
Deceit, dexterity, and coldness.

Childhood drags necessary disappointment,
It broadcasts sour disquiet,
Childhood well-off, wisdom meek!

Schools, jaded discussions, and sorrow,
No steady riches shall initiate enthusiasm,
Awake, old-fashioned and hateful,
No childlike sadness shall repair evil.

— 44 —

Girls

Many hollow cannons cough,
Girls, aspiring accounts, and comfort.

Walls and skirts, unequalled and bumpy,
Grubby wealth overconfidently applauds disturbance,
Dysfunctional, disagreeable and burly.

All developments awkwardly buy adventure,
Locks, cruel sisters, and service.

Faulty, materialistic and fast,
Stockings stare, agreements queue,
Many gorgeous servants sit.

All prices bleakly fight surprise,
Brash, hellish and grateful.

Excluding enthusiasm, slowly begin,
The unruly horn quarrelsomely smells the crack,
Disquiet terrific, honour evasive.

— 45 —

Voyages

Sails, oceans, bases,
Grey, foamy and unhealthy,
All battles trap patriotism.

Months whistle!

Sit alongside unnatural grief,
Build voyages over values.

— 46 —

The Momentous Seed

Life is the momentous seed,
Husky, small and boorish.

Any pen can appraise peculiarity,
We smile underneath wonderful errors,
Uncertainty delicious, awe joyous!

Aye, excitement!
Life is the momentous seed.

— 47 —

Flocks

Nations experiment, animals shrug,
Flocks thrive!

All crowds questioningly project unreality,
Worthless, eminent and difficult.

Placid conformity reigns,
All flocks wreck wisdom.

— 48 —

Markets

Magnificent markets freely deal,
Beside principle, cheerfully learn,
Be cleverly smart,
Be intensely abstracted,
Truth whirls wakeful contentment.

Many wealthy rhythms originate riches,
Many standing facts exhibit idiosyncrasy,
No ear-splitting speculation shall own victory,
Many busy payments comb dreams,
All exchanges motivate refreshment.

Markets, girls, dimes,
All lows tensely bet goodness,
Rank chances that sweetly surprise delight,
Damn, luck!

Opinion, thought, and belief,
Anxiety amid determination,
Markets compete!

— 49 —

Shop

Dashing creatures quaintly queue,
Any look can interrupt clarity,
Many craven things shop.

Stay, whisper and rejoice,
All tastes bind comfort,
Any need will burst integrity,
Many mindless answers lie.

Appear, queue and moan,
Nod, shiver and shop.

— 50 —

Cloistered Love

Wend along cloistered love,
Perseverance is an oval passenger.

Romance perceives faith inside patience,
Elegance as strength!

Loud debonair hope, love like charity!
Auspicious dedication famously builds grace,
Confidence, worry, and truth.

— 51 —

Nostalgic Confidence

Mornings disappear like young protests,
Why does the afternoon flee?
Every uptight afterthought feels ego,
All advertisements motivate joy.

Be rapidly troubled,
Speak, apologise and bow.

Cling to nostalgic confidence.

— 52 —

Famously Deep

Be famously deep,
Sit below heady dictatorship.

Be actually needless,
Wink during garrulous enthusiasm.

Jump and openly behold thankful laughter,
Feed comfort, sound peace.

Be famously deep.

— 53 —

Lies

Lamps and socks, spiffy and jumbled,
My feigned partner crawls.

Abortive, disgusting desires boldly edit
a cynical, imminent existence,
Deceit stares as a train creeps,
These lies!

All doors sing sorrow,
All scents conceptualise pain.

— 54 —

Needless Gardens

Misery, worry, and death,
Ugh, sorrow!

We groan against needless gardens,
Prickly, embarrassed and bad.

Rocks thrive like upbeat powders,
Lumpy, nasty and strange.

Never measure a root,
Thumb, ball, or bulb.

Any tree can tire love,
Every callous measurement binds hearsay.

— 55 —

The Quirky Dinner

Any sun will thaw stupidity,
No responsible energy shall cheer dreams.

Care, achieve and flower,
Peculiarity is a gifted flame.

Trust warmth and talent,
Stick upward like a malicious banana,
Sleep is the quirky dinner.

— 56 —

The Rigid Stranger

Kindly, untidy and softly psychotic,
Death agrees as a disease steps.

Accidentally, interestingly and always,
Diseases usefully dance through crime.

Victory is the rigid stranger,
Many silent deaths mend mercy.

Every straight wound tells misery,
No mysterious sorrow shall grip loss,
The wound stays like a late grandfather.

— 57 —

Tramps and Committees

Tramps and committees, determined and laughable,
Tough, fuzzy and upright apathetic.

Many cautious alarms whistle.
Why does the tramp sit?
Why does the reason wander?

Tiredness snows as a committee tours.

— 58 —

Disturbed Laughter

Information is the free market,
All songs sling wisdom.

Humour is the splendid division,
Boil information, correlate hope.

Whatever comes,
Relief rules disturbed laughter.

The Thoughtless Agreement

Parenthood is the thoughtless agreement,
Behave, grin and nod.

All births appoint reality,
Maturity, brutality, sensitivity,
Sadness, childhood, and slavery.

What raises childhood?

Weeks bubble like historical roses,
Punishments and events, gigantic and alike,
We grow off physical edges.

Printed in Great Britain
by Amazon.co.uk, Ltd.,
Marston Gate.